A Time To Awaken

By Bernard Ballard

These poems are to be read aloud

ISBN: 978-0-9979008-5-9
Cover Illustration By Gabriella Mitchell
Formatted by Nancy Cates
Published by Bernard Ballard
Email----Ballardbernard584@gmail.com

EKPHRASTIC POETRY
(Wisdom Writings)

Poems in Rhyme and Riddle
Unravel The Unsolvable Riddle

(meditations for awakening)

**What are the questions answered in these poetic riddles?
Formulate four questions that must be asked to solve the riddle
hidden in the poem.**

Who, why, when, where?

What does it mean?
What does it seem?
What is it being?

Definitions

1. Spirit Being Born
Before the separation, before judgment, before birth.

2. Silent Night
Everything is Light projected. Every thing in this form-based physical reality is a product of the Mind. Staying present, and realizing this, is the way to true peace, and joy in living.

3. Second Chance
You can only know the true nature of life by experiencing it. You only appreciate the nature of forgiveness by having experienced it's opposite.

4. Re-find Out
We enter into this dream reality to experience the opposites, to challenge self to find again what's real and true.

5. Quantum Quiet Guest
Who is he who fell asleep, forgetting who he is, in order to experience life in form?

6. Place Of Fear Mongers
A metaphysical representation of our life in dreams as we begin awakening. The only power in fear is your belief in it.

7. Who Fell Asleep
You are light born of time and space experiencing through a process of imagining a perceived reality born of thoughts made manifest. A dream in time.

8. Way Of Fools
This world is a product of thought. Truth can only be known by going beyond the realm of thought.

9. Perception That's Projected
Truth can only be found by going inside. Into that still silence, the core of your being.

10. Look Beyond This Land
Those who live from the point of view achieved by the intellect cannot see the deeper truth beneath the surface meaning .

11. Flavored Lies
The truth about this world of form and the intellect, or ego mind.
We are created as the One, and journey into separation thoughts and beliefs until we waken from the dream. The lies or untruths that you are taught and believe, that keep you trapped and ignorant of your true reality.

12. Less Than He
You can never be less than you were created to be.

13. I Am Not Afraid
A reason for conscious awakened being to live in this illusory reality. Why living life your own way is better than following rules and laws. The Ones who know, return to teach the children, to grow out of doubt and ignorance. Following rules in books will keep you from finding your own way.

14. I Dreamed before
Can truth be known by human beings? A look at our experience from a different perspective.

15. Eternal Enmity
Peace can only be known and experienced in the present. Nowhere else can it be found.

16. From Photons
We are beings of light.

18. Bespeak, Believe Will Be
What you believe in your heart, and speak with your mind is become this life experience in earth. Change your belief, and change the experience of life on earth.

19. Truth From Lies
Do you live your life from a place of peace, or is it fear that guides your actions. Do you truly believe the things that you have accepted as truth to live by? Do you believe this world to be a reflection of the thoughts and feelings of the masses?

20. The One Pretending
You cannot be the one that you pretend to be.

21. Told The Tale
This life experience is a tale, a dream. It is made from thoughts and beliefs.

22. State Of Singleness
Every thing is interconnected. Everything is a part of the One. Change one thing, one idea, one concept and see the whole begin to reflect that thought. A new world thus begins.

23. Mind Divide To Achieve
You create this world to have a place to experience the power of your thoughts, through dreamed illusions that aren't real. Do you follow your inner guidance, or do you live according to the things believed and taught by this world?

A Time To Awaken

A key to the apprehension of the concepts presented in these works is an impossible idea, which supposedly occurred before the beginning of time. It goes like this:

(from -A Course in miracles)
Into eternity there crept a (tiny mad idea) at which the Son of God forgot to laugh. In his forgetfulness did the thought become a serious idea, and possible of both accomplishment and real effects.

This idea is a perception of the mind, and is the cause of all the so called evil that exist. To correct this idea is to return to a way of being that is joy, peace, and abundance.

Perception
 All perception is a product of thinking. From thinking we "are" our minds, we begin to see that we have minds, and that it is the mind that has thoughts, beliefs, feelings and concepts.

There are many important questions that must be asked, and answered in order to realize your truth. That is the purpose of these writing. You might call them myth, a dream, and illusion, a perceptual imagined reality based in relativity. It is all we have, here and now, to deal with, to uncover, and in so doing make life a joy instead of a drudgery

The mystic proclaims:

Our mind is our home in which we live and manifest this world.
As we clean up the microcosm in our mind, then the macrocosm, the world will clear up also.

Contents

Spirit Beings Born

The monkey sat up on the fence
deciding just which way they went

to find this diamond, cast in time

when everything was made to shine.
From sheep to goats, they are the same.
An animal defined to tame

or keep as house pets, and to drain
their energies, so we explain
that after school we felt the same

as monkey men were trained to tame
all of their natural desires
and live in cages, that's the same

as spirit beings born of earth

found out, that seems to do the same
because they are taught from their youth
to never sit, to never stay

in silent stillness, and to pray

with words that only cause delay.
Explaining what they think to know.

They pass over, that which shall know
them into beings that can't die
but do pretend to be the lie
taught in the books that make the same

mistake to try and re-explain

what can't be taught, or told, or shown
to those who live by senses known
to only perceive what is seen
and felt, and touched as what you need

to have to show it is alive
when angels know that I can't die
for I'm created just as He.

By that which is the life of me.

For how can One that's whole and real
be seen as just what image be
designed to walk the land, and pass
like rain to mist, and rock to sand.

It all does change in time, in time
you'll understand you are divine.
Once you have tired of playing games
though you can star, and take no blame.

Silent Night

And so I write it once again.

These sayings that always begin
inside a mind that has defined
it's task to run, and play a day

or two, outside the gloom that proved

to be the one thing any fool
might follow too, to find a way
out of, around this day by day.

My living in a way that says.

I cannot be afraid to stay
in present moment where I say
the one thing that is true today

and grows, becomes the kind of day

where I feed all my appetites
with vegetables that no one may
accuse, and make me go astray.

For living in the kind of way
I chose ten thousand years ago
when we first found the way back in

to living dear, without the fear

that we had failed to notice while
we were involved in going round
to find another we could blame.

For all the things that do enflame

and claim another is the One
responsible for what I feel

or what to do while being attacked
by all the doubts and fears I share
about the One who made this fair

to be a play, where all forgot.

It's just in time, where we can rhyme

addition into multiples
which illustrate the ways we find
our way back out of alleys blocked.

To keep up, in this way of being
that no way sane, can ere escape.

To see the Light of Truth abides
in all who drop their innocent
appeals to stand, and to deny

that anything we think, we do
and all the things we thought are done.

No, not to you or any One
who stands and watches without fear

and sees these mountains come apart
to reveal light is always part
of everything that's born to die

in this imagined world where I
create these things that seem mistakes
but that's impossible to make.

Cause everything has a beginning

in the mind, that's based in fear
or happiness that shows, the cheer
and fearlessness you posed to show.

That, what is thought must one day come
to you, and me, and everyone
who thinks he's free to live and be.

The thing that he does call himself.

To see in others, just the self
that he imagines in his dream
that mirrored image that tells me.

I am the One you chose to see
and delved into, so you might be
the One forgives, and gives the key

of Loving all that he does see

in silent nights when he believes
that he recalls, and does belong
in innocence, that does prove he

Is one with All that Is, can beam.

Once all divisions are perceived
to be a way to find his way
back into the belief that he

might take one step, and see it's just.

The only way to find your way
back home to when this all began
and ends.

Second Chance

I'm hot again, so tell me friend
about this man that I pretend
is All, that I claimed I could be

before I found out it is we

who found the most in fairies land
where it takes two to do a thing
in lives that struggle to be One

who tells the truth to everyone.

Who stands out on his own and claims.
I only do that which I am.
The one survived this chain of fools

that I've pretended night and day

for oh, so long that I can say.
It can't be me, beneath that tree
of saturated lies that buy

the idea that I am why
this all has come about today
to show me just might not

be delayed
another day but faced right now.

Admitting what it is I fear.

Then stepping into all the gust
of wind, that bends my mind around
to see, just what it was I say

became of truth, became of love

when I began to celebrate
the days of old when we were gay
enough to celebrate it all.

Down to the times when I seemed us.
Down to the false self I proclaimed
could not be blamed for what he is

but simply learn how not to live

to gain those things that never last
'til summer time does come at last
to show you all that you have gained

or lost, if you decide to blame
another for the way you feel

or felt about the lives you've lived.
Learning about, without a doubt

what brings down, what left you us

is just to know that it is thus
the way we learn how to forgive
ourselves for playing parts that tame

and show that no one is to blame
for living life inside this glass.
Half filled with all that's diced

and spread upon the floor to life.

To show you just how that advice
received, and given to the wind
might just return to you again.

A second change for you to win
the prize held out that transcends doubt
about that thing you had become

just playing out these roles that come

together, just to show you how
we all must live to give us true
the things we realize show you.

That just because you took the road

that only leads you to fool's gold
does your life, ever stand as less
or more than you do now caress

who you are here, and you are now.

So let go all that you have found
to simplify your way was found
to be exactly what you needed

to demonstrate we all have wings
were hidden well until the day
we have experienced all that formed

inside this realm where everything
is just your dreams come to abide
and demonstrate your state of mind.

Re-find Out

I'm up again to pretend friend
to be the One that I intend
to become now, and then again.

I don't believe in making trends.

By being that, another thing
that I set out to do at first
in the beginning of the jest.

To find a way to re-find out

this story told around the world
of iron bars that keep me in
this false mind-set that has begun

to run its course, to be, of course.

The only thing that could become
or try to find out, why and when
I came into this same old space.

Not growing up to mind my pace

might lead me to another term
or take me out beyond the dunes
where objects do not have to fight

or struggle just to say, I'm right

in time with you, in tune with fools
who don't believe in making gains
who are content to be the same

as, which stood out ten thousand games

of "I don't know", and "I can't do".

Yet I go round and round like fools
do when the world does spin and spin
the same old tune, to show your friend

that time and space is just a place.

That mirrors what you think is right
that mirrors what you believe true
that reflects all the things you do.

Inside your mind, your energies
are dueling, to make amends
to show and tell your 'self what can.

Cannot be, the jest of when
you finally open up your mind

to see if maybe it can find
a way out of this same old space
been visited again to waste
your time.

Quantum Quiet Guest

The time has come to stop the play
and let your mind go far, a way
from here and now, to "I don't know"

the reasons I've created hell
except to punish what is wrong

or right those things that have become
the idle moments where I say
that life is fair enough today.

For here and now is all I have

or ever will, in time to kill
these lies about a future time
when all our lives, and all our friends

will be united once again.
To start again, this play again
where we act out the things believed.

Not knowing it is he, not me

who fell asleep, and dreams these dreams
where I pretend to be what's not
where I profess to not know what
I am, or what I came to do.

For that would spoil all the fun
in make believing, that does come
from ignorance of what I am

and where I came from to begin.

This end game, which does tell the tale

that has been made to keep us well
beneath the surface of this lie
about a man, who could not die.

For he is not of bone and flesh.

He is a quantum quiet guest

of what appears inside this dream-
like fantasy that's so extreme
that any fool can play the part

of One, who claims he is not smart
enough to know that God's can't lie
or make mistakes, or try to make

our lives so pitifully hell.

They are much bigger than we tell
ourselves to believe specks of sand
could cause a mountain top to stand

and cry and lie, and kill and steal
away from Love, and caring deals
which dictate he forgive them all.

For trying things you do recall

that no one knows a thing at all
until he walked the line, and call
or claimed that now I know the true

way that's for One, and why I be.

The wisdom that accrues around
the One who don't act like a clown
believing what he reads in books

because his parents, and these crooks
who run time's world, who make it swirl

around, and for six thousand years
until we see there is no cheer
in waiting, for the Savior's come

into our lives to show us, from
the only thing that we need come
to understand, there's only One

in quantum microscopic sum.

Place of Fear Mongers

Tonight we stop our running way
and join with others I do say
who are the willing Ones who come

away from safe and satisfied.

Who are the Ones, who do choose to
stand up, and make a brand new tale.
One where I stand with hand and tail

attending to my 'Self to show.
I love me, and this shadow's show.

Which is the opposite of what
I found to be no safer than
ignoring signs and signals to

abandon all those foolish rules

which take you back, that tell you that
you are not free, and cannot see
and find the good out for yourself

from what distracts from growing back

to trusting in your choices made
that may take you a different way
than what the law of license tells.

Of what not trusting in yourself
will lead you to an emptiness
which can't be born or told.

For what it truly represents.

The fear of failure that has spent

you in this place of fear mongers
who never dare to skip and jump

with joy, because the books do say.

That pleasure puts you in the way
of wild dogs, who can never tell.
The smell of fish from dried up lips

repeat the same old songs again.

The same Ones that don't give a damn
where babies first lay down, and tell
these stories are not ever what

is real, and true but just reflect
the that, we do choose to bare where
we don't face up to what is there

is like to test your willingness
to just accept it as it comes

to simply know it's all a dream.

That you create it all yourself.

To show and tell your old beliefs.
I have a brand new way to see
where dancing is okay to do.

Who love of All That Is, denies:

That truth, that there's a special One
The fact that there's only one way.
The lie that's made us all to die
believing we are only part.

Believing we can break a law
that stands the test, that is the best
and only thing you have to do

is trust your intuition, come

to show you how to overcome
this fear that's real as I believe
in what I choose to make, and see.

Who Fell Asleep

Now, how do I do anything
except to sit upon this stone
of iron, born of meteors
that stuck together for a fling

around this universe of One.

Where everything began as One
Light born of time, and out of Space
t'was settled and began this race

of men was manifested from.

The idea that we can't be One
but twos, and threes, and fours become
the form filled place that thinks, and comes

apart to live in life, and die
for all things false must re-become
because they're really only One.

One Light, One Way, One everyone

who all appear inside this Light
who just for spite, or fun insights
the sky that don't exist no more

as empty space for that is for

the formless that has birthed this world
into the nations that are for
the intellect to manage well

enough to judge, and make believe

that there's a better, or a worse.
That there's a here and over there
that time and space, they are the dance
believed by all the sleeping Ones.

Who dream these dreams to re-become.

To gain advantage and become
the rulers of this place where fun
was made to be, yet now becomes

a place of war where things exist

for man to best, and become rich
enough to play the all fall down
from knowing all of us are One

who fell asleep to dream this dream

that maybe seems, and maybe beams
a scent of true, or make believe
depends on where you're looking from.

Up high above, or down below
these ideas and concepts flow
to form what's seen and thus believed

to be what's real, and what is true
or is it all just made belief

by fallen giants who've become
so dense in intellect, that's come
away from truth, and light, and love

to measure all for what it's worth
to mortal man, that kind of land

that thinks he's better than the rest
because he thinks, and yes he plans
to make this earth a better place

then it is here and it is now.

The way that Source had made it be
to play around, and see if He

can re-remember back again
out of the form that knows it can
deep down inside become the end
begun in Light that has not been.

Way Of Fools

I'm flying way up high again
although I cannot tell my friend
the rhythm that I feel in here

or in my mind, which I can find
whenever I get up from sleep

and take my time to see if we
might go again out in the storm
of life, and love all that we find

will be exactly as refined

the day we all did hold our breath
for long enough to ever guess
again, why it is all so long

since we first took that first long step
into this place where we forget
the facts of life do not make sense

unless you look from deep within

the reasons that you claim my friend
is living in this world of form
where everything is by design

provided that you never find

the reason it was all thought up
to keep you safe inside this bowl
of memories that can't be found

except in present moment now.

What you believe will come to you
and all those others gathered round
to hold up all that you were taught

to never look this way or that

but follow in the way of fools
who never seem to know what's real
and yet they are the last to fast

from folly which is what we do
when we depend on others who

have been this way a time before

discovered it is nothing more
than what you say, and do believe
will come about, and be made real

in fantasy adventures will
not let you sleep for ever now.

For it's the only place or time
where you determine just which rhyme
will come to life, will be made real
in melodies that some say kill

the truth that it is all made up
by fearing what is here and now.
Which cannot be imagined, how

tomorrow, or that yesterday

you mixed up, and did cause delay
to all who look both back and forth
to find what can, will never be

appreciated here and now.

Cause that's not what it's meant to do
in day and night where I tell you
these tales of horror, or of bliss
which you pretend helps you to kiss

the lips of Mother Earth's divine
ability to finally find
the reasons that we've all come here

to live these lives to redefine
that facts, that never last too long
in generations when these Songs

of Solomon were played so loud
that all the children dropped their nets

well filled with so much fish we left
this dreaming dreams that only seem
to make up for our past delights

to become what is out of sight

to all that have not closed the door
on doubt and fear, of ups and downs
and accept it is all a dream come true.

Perception That's Projected

These imaged ideas come through
to me
because I've found a different way.

To go inside, and stop my mind
from playing all those old dead tapes
about its friend who is not well

enough, so that he ever tells

the fairies stories aren't from hell
or heaven, for it is to me
a guiding light to show the way

to see this life as if it's me

who hold the ties, and says goodbye
to all the old and tried that failed
to take me to a place of joy.

Where good and bad, they are the same.

Just points on different parts of a
perception that's projected out

agreeing with the world or not.
It doesn't matter to the One

whose closed his eyes, and goes inside
to see and hear these visions glide
to anyone whose made mistakes.

I tell you they do build the case

to prove what it is, right and true
or filled with what does not serve you
or anyone who takes this run

in form, to see what it might be
to separate these ideas bent
on proving something other can't

be told a way that does provide

the kind of deal that I declare
must be the one to suit my fair
and different ways to find my way

not following another One.

Except when we might see the same
and know that all ways go the same
because beginnings always end.

In ways that can't be told or said
to idiots, who life had lead
down roads that show you can't get free

while doing what another deems

is right for you, is good for two
or three, or more cause we're the same
just choosing to be what we dare.

In fear, or loathing of what may
be just a plan to keep us here

in ignorance because the fear
of others who are sleepwalking
can never deem a way to say

what isn't, and what ain't, they say

the way to find your way back home.

It's in the future, they all say
for past time heros know the way

that got them in, and took them down
a road that seemed to come out free

but had to die, to know if he

had found that way, and any way
for all those children gone a way

that must be followed or denied
to be what's real, and true to do.
To find the way that always says.

That is what life is for.

Look Beyond This Bend

I've finally found a way to sing
these melodies which all do ring

inside the Silence of the Lamb

inside my mind where I do find
that space, that is not space at all
that place, that isn't here and now

that open door, where all we see
the sights that no one will believe

from earth suits, which are made to hide

the deeper things that do reside
in formless realms where it declares
the messages that can't be told

to fools whose folly won't behold

what lies beyond the intellect
which is what isn't, and what ain't
described in wholly books that won't

allow you freedom to be here
and do the things that you declare
might not be written in that book
may not be seen, or even liked

by men who claim to know it all.

The every verse, and voice that says.
Don't do, and do forgive the Ones

who bowl down too, and pay their tithes

to keep their demon minds in check

from knowing what would truly bless
us all to know the way behind
those open doors no one can find.

For least you look beyond this land
you'll never find that peace which lands
you in a place which has no form.

Not folly found that might let clowns
believing someone else can do
forgiveness to, forgiveness for
their error thought, which won't be lost

until they stand up and be boss
of all their guilt, and all the shame
they share when they believe in lame

ideas that claim a man can sin

against a Love, that don't begin
in separation thought created
just to claim that God would judge

and blame, and claim there is a hell

created by some nasty snails
that can't get up, that won't stand still
and hear the sound of one hand clapping
in and out of voids foretold

to Holy men who do behold
the truth that all that's real is God.
The fact that there's no other side.
The fantasy dissolved away

to reveal truth has always stayed
in present moment which is now.
The day that you have finally found
there is no past or future told.

For only here and now are real.

Life to life

The wind blew hard upon the rope
that I held on, to stay afloat
in lightning flashes topped the houses
out beside the hills below.

I knuckled under pressure held
onto, until I felt the dread

of waking up, or going back
to sleep, where I was living dead.

Without the stained glass windows formed
that dedicated, made my dorm
look like a shadow from the night

where I forgot to turn on Light

that had been hidden, buried deep
inside this place I call the Keep.

And kept it does, my secrets well
enough that I no longer tell
my family the stories known

before I became overgrown
to life in form, that seems so real

that all my neighborhoods are still.

The reason that I return here
from life to life so I can cheer.

My failure and successes all

make me behold the reason for

forgiving life for being me.

The One, at last, who holds the key
to setting all the captives free
from long held false beliefs that kill

desire, to be well and good.
No matter what we think we should.

Be strong or weak. Be all that we
achieve once we believe that She
and He are parts of what is whole.

The feminine, that once did show
the traits of Mother Nature's swells.
She creates what we once deemed hell.

A place to go, and come, and know.

Discover what we always were
or what we thought we could not be
in flesh and blood, not like a tree

which stays connected to its root
and leaves, it knows are part of He

who is the All that Is, or was

assembled as it is the who
of life on earth and everywhere.

The dreamscape can never be fair.
For it is filled with opposites.
To test, and see if you can tell

the true, or else believe the lie
that we are blind, we cannot die.

For consciousness transcend this form
of nightmare mirror images
that swear
all that you see, or smell, or touch
are just vibrations that have touched

your mind in deeper furrows than
the true ones that had first been planned

to give you just a taste of fun

and see if you can overcome
that lie, and doubts that you do shout
out in your night of sleep, to see.

If all the world is blind as well.
If all this world can't even tell
the opposite of truth are nots.

The opposite of form is light.

The opposite of wrong is right
behind your eyelids which attach
the true way, that we all can know
once we slowdown, and do what shows

that one times one, times one is One.

There's only One that has become
the long forgotten prodigal
who lost his way, so he could say

I've done it all in shadow form

not nothing can compare to dorms
where we lay down and close our eyes.
Where we begin to visualize

or forgive it, and let it go.

That new creations can be birthed
inside this life which is exact.

Just what you choose to believe real.

So try your best not to forget.
It all begins and ends in time.
That can't exist unless you've space

to find your mind to be divine.

You need only believe, and taste
the glory of the human race
which shows all that we do esteem.

Inside these dreams we do believe

that adding up is better than
the multiplying of the Lamb
that knows that all of us are One

Cause, one times one, times one is One.

Less Then He

Now Close your mouth, or you will see
the things that I will do to he
who opens up his head held high

to demonstrate the reason why

he thinks that he has come from high
above the One, who stooped so low
that they did enter here, so slow
that everything seemed made of gold

but looks, do never tell you how

or when, or why it all had been
a scene was never seen before
or heard of, out beyond the moors

where settlements were made to take

away your pride, and by and bye,
you taught that it was you, not eye
who made the plan, opened the land

to all the lies and doubts abide
where ever you do think that you
are less then He created you

to be the One who never runs
but stands so still, he never will

have need to call his brothers cold
or bold enough to give it up.

That thing, that all mankind has been

before it learned to settle in
to ways that prove it never left

or lost its way in spite of why

the old folk prayed they'd never go

or find their own way, which would win
the honorary seat upon
the dais that no One here can bare

or care to follow in a way

that follows in the rules that say
what is, or isn't a delight
to those who've learned to never fight

to be the best, or be seen less
then we all know, before we go
into these idle forms that flow

and follow in the way that goes

another way which may delay
the ripening of fruit left high
enough upon that tree that blooms

only, when it is time for him

to take his stand, to make demand
of all is known, and thought to be
the cherished settled way to see

that it has always been with thee.

For you are One who lost his way

to find and know he had become
the only way that's known to stay
in peace, and love, and grace today.

I'm Not Afraid

The little children of this world
are the one thing worth living for.

Outside the rainbows in our eyes
which keep us all in ways despised
by all the Ones who've gone and come

back into being, to see some

of you decide to re-divide
your purpose, and to then abide
in ways that make the lightning strike
the mountains, and cause them to quake

to open out their bowl, and sound
like trumpets, before a true tale

is told to only those who grow
away from doubt, and ignorance
that holds the human race in chains

so willing are they to be trained.

They obey laws that don't make sense.
They follow rules made up to bend
them back in line, so they can't find
the only thing worth living for

is knowing who you are, and why
you've come into this ancient door

to realize it is a shame

to never raise your eyes and say

I'm not afraid. I dare to do.

I care enough for me and you
to solve the riddles made in life

which puzzle all the intellect

which can't see out beyond the doors

that they keep closed, so they can mourn
the infantile way that they live
in houses that no dollhouse claims

could ever hold the gems and pearls
that fall from skies that have deployed
the righteous way, which is to know.

Your choice is all that's best for you.

To do, to learn a different way
or maybe not, it could delay
your progress to what does feel real.

But then at least you know for sure

which way it is for you to come
or not return this way again.

Now how can laws and rules show that.

They only keep you in the back
of those who choose the lies to lead
the foolish Ones, afraid to live

or grow, or know just who they are

and why, they came here to find cheer.
In ventures that reveal the truth
only to those who hold to youth.

I dreamed before

The angels all come home at night
to be in place, to stay in place
where they may never be again

and this can only be explained

by those who don't believe the lies
by those who failed to realize
by those content to be the best

of all the Ones who dared to care

about the way it was before
we chose this path where we are more
than men who open wide the door

than those who fold their hands and play

in circles where without delay
their memory returns to be
in present moment where we see

that all that ever was or is
existent in these walls and drawers

is elemental to the facts
is just a way to show-off lack
of knowing what you knew before

you chose to come into the core
of wild ideas flung about
to demonstrate all that is back

of images that are a place
and part in this the human race.

To find what isn't, and yet is
a platitude that might be said
to be the place where all forgot.

That rain and wind come from the same.
That sun and moon might take the blame
that I am not the way I came

but visualized from out of stars

that help us see we aren't from Mars
or Venus, or none of the rest
of planets made to add, to test

our stories which exist in time

and space creates enormous place

to film these reels of I am not
the One who could ever forget
that in this moment All in all

is happening to help console

the visions that I dreamed before
I lost the thing that might explain
that all I am, or ever can

belongs to that, will not exclaim.

It's better, or it's worse to do.

What freedom teaches is the truth
of power that's no force at all
but imitates from what can't be

inside a world where all things are

run by these forces, non can bar
or find the final reason why
or see beyond that open door

or raise above the" I can do"
whatever freedom tells you to
remember, we are made to be
free agents to believe, and be

or simply know, and stay so still

so no one round the monster will
beware of what goes on in camps
where visibility is key

to all who play around the bush
of "I don't know"{, and I don't care
to step out of this house of straw
It makes it easy when I fall.

To blame the others who are there
to take the blame, so I can fair
a day or two, perhaps a year
in golden rings, and keys to see.

This venture as the one I chose
to have, so I won't have to go
back to the place I chose to leave

a moment, so that I can see

the wonderment I have achieved
to waken from, or re-believe.

Eternal Enmity

The dreamtime has come over me.
Its taking me, its bringing me
into a way can't be conceived

from where I've lived in time, before

I wakened fully from the scenes
that I invented for to last
and task myself to find myself

in realm, that play the "I forgot"

to tell myself to find some rest
in only one way it can be
in all the ways were said to be

but was that not the way we fell?

By following up hill and dale
instead of being where we are
observing all that goes around

and round until, we did fall down

avoiding what is here and now
because it did not feel as sweet
or taste as good as golden wheat

that had been bred to keep up down
until the wheels that go around
were lost to what is real and true.

The center that is out of bounds

to all who seek to find that land
where hands are clapping all the time.

Where one eye shuts to re-combine

those half truths that we knew before
we opened up, and closed that door

where all the others stored their stories
made to keep us company.
Until eternal enmity
might set us free, or let us go

into that time that's without space

into that space where no Ones race.
From here to there or anywhere
but holds their ground without a rhyme.

To follow in the way to past
or future goals, for we all know.
There's only here and now.

From Photons

I'm seated here inside this light.

It used to make me feel a fright.
But now, when I am all alone
I know that it does take me home

to reason, what is here and now.

Before my eye, though I don't know
or understand these things that come
and go, and sometimes make me run

like mad men do before they come
to sanity, and know what some
that could not find their way back home

and returned to that place where dumb
is well accepted by those cons
to intellectuality
which sums

all that a man from earth can know
or believe in, that keeps him from
the truer wisdom that abides
deep down inside, below the cum.

That makes us think that flesh and bone
is all we are, is where we're from.

But that's a belief that is from
a time when we believed we're from
a place in time and space that dates

back to Newtonian physics.

Before they split the atom up
and found it's made of particles
that are composed of photons, yet.

They have no mass, that is a fact.

That all you see, and all you be
originates where you can't see
with intellectual beliefs.

That satisfied the priest and chiefs
that hid the older knowledge well
from all the poor folk who excel

in innocence, and ignorance
of intuitions that they sell

as superstitious lies that sell
you hell, and call you demon spells
to keep you lost in fairy tales

about a God who never tells

you stories in these dreams esteemed
to be the real that you are, cells

arise inside your consciousness.

As if you're lost to all that fell
apart when you believed these tales
told by the ones created hell

to keep you bound in fear, and tell
these stories guaranteed to sell

you on the lies, and all the truths

invented down beneath your cell.

In dungeons have been well concealed
by all this world which testifies
that you are flesh, and you are blood.

You cannot be a god disguised.

You cannot be the first born Son.
Cause you're a sinner, and you've come

to live a little while and die.
To make your babies for a while
and never think that you are from.

These lighted particles that come

from photons, and that is the sum
of all I know about the from.

Flavored Lies

And then the magic of the glen
came spilling down around, and bound

me to the way I was before
this world was born, became forlorn
as all the others felt to be.

In ways that prove, that what you see
can't be no more than flavored lies

which you create to show me I

am born in memory of light
that slay the opposite belief.

That they who roam the hills and dales
alone were guaranteed to fall
and moan
because no reason ever comes
to those who make their own way home.
To those who dared to take the chance

known well by all those others who
would not believe the lies and doubts
we worshipped, once we fell asleep

that made us all appear as sheep

lined up to see their families
and kin, and fellow beings slain
for following the way that truth

must lead all those engaged in life.
That has no pattern, shows no plan

that can be captured inside books.

For once you know the way of kings
you do not have to re-pretend.
You'll never need to ask a thing

or follow lines that are defined
by rules and regulations meant
to leave you far away from home.

Designed to glide in, out of all
that you do need to see, and be.

The being you're made up to be

in time and space, that can't neglect
it's intellect, the way it thinks
believing that is all there is.

To master life, to be the spice
that seasons all the Master made.
That tops the dishes can't be dreamed

by those refusing life again
to living in the mirrored shed

that looks so comfortable, we shed
our truthed ideas, which were made
in laboratories made of blood

and mixed up flesh that never could

reveal the light that stars expose
to raise the lilies up at night
that cause the swans to all take flight

and rainbows double in the skies

that all did seem to re-deny

what can't be spoken, can't be known
without the innocent below
those stairs that climbed to opened lairs.

When beast were trapped and set on fire
to purify, and thus deny
all of the things that we had taught

accepted as the way to see
and hold the darkened knight achieved
in dreams we worshipped as our cause.

Bespeak, Believe Will Be

It's here again, and I do bend
my pen around, and do begin
to write again, I do begin
this rhyme to show I am your friend

or I am not the kind of man
who takes up with the kind of band
that stands around, and will not bend
the will, to do the things it can.

To make a difference in this land
where everything does seem the same
where everything does take the name
that you bespeak, believe will be.

The title that it holds today
in realms that play the tune that may
be seen, and heard a thousand years

by all who stand inside, and cheer

these elements of thought, that vote
to be, and do the things you see
inside your mind, you do conceive

of things have never been before

you came to life, were born again
to new ideas that "I can"
and will allow my hand to bend

away from ideas they called sin.

In days when ignorance began

to replace all that could begin
to take us out of those crude ways
that always did cause us to say

the things that judgment brings about.

The lowering of all that's thought
to be the true way that we go
to lift up all that don't belong
in minds that serve the way of peace.

In minds that make this world at least

by belief systems that are part
of what's been taught to all who start
there education in a way
where they do believe all that say.

What's true is what the papers say

or what's heard on the news today.
You cannot go with what you see
and think inside a mind that bends
ideas round, and turns a part

of silent stillness to its mark
of revelating in the way
it always does where you just say...

Reveal to me the way today.
That I would see, and be, and do
the highest things that I might choose.
The best thing that is right to do

for all that may, for all I say

be able to know, be and do
comes out from stillness that includes
all things that move, and sing, and say.

The difference that's left inside
in miracles that don't divide
a thing, but lets it all implode
into the beginning of mad

ideas that the pilgrims bring
with them, into this dream that can
be changed around, be made a new.
A different way to show the clues

will bring us round to sanity
and saner ways to be and see
that after all is said and done.
No one can tell you where to run.

Just close your eyes while you decide
to follow in the way of kings
who all ways get what they believe
will come around, will come back to

cause laws of physics always do
maintain in true, and wisdom deeds
that do not believe what you see
but are the opposite, in fact.

Do, do create what you believe
to be the real and true that starts
as you begin to draft new charts
that show a different way to see.

And be and go, so others needs
are not your own responsibility.

If you would take that first long step
to let them be, to let them go
their way, for they are choices made
within your mind and heart to stay

within this dream that you have dreamed

to illustrate that you are smart
enough to follow in the way
that you must go, you need to stay
on track with your responsibility.

Is to be silent if you see
that playing in around these ponds
that do surround this infinite ground

will change them all, will draw them in
to see, and be the image seen
in your imagination beams

with lovely light which give them freedom
to begin their lives again
in ways without your judgments sway.

To tell them there's a better way
to be, and do inside this land

that they do claim it, all I am
inside this bowl of jelly stands
or sets inside the kind of mind

that worries not, but knows that time
is here and now, believed or not

allowed to set, and root, and grow
up out of lies that had been told.
Yet lost their strength in times you bend
to hearing things from out the void.

That silent place in stillness knows.
It's all a dream that you have made.

Believing this, you take the spade
and dig a little deeper, next
time you decide that it is best
to lend to your own mind, and find.

That others can believe and know
more than it seems, more than you deemed.

To trust the Universe to give
them just exactly what they live
inside this realm where we all do
the things that we believe can be.

And know inside, deep down inside
that all is well and good.

Truths From Lies

This world of life is filled with bums
who do not know where they've come from.
They live to die, and die to live.

To go to heavens in the sky

where no one knows that we all know.
No, not a thing about the lie.

Foretold in all the tales 'bout whales
and ships that sink to bring the goal
of all of us who want to know

yet do not care if it is fair
or false, so long as we don't dare
to enter into ways of fear.

That guarantees we only hear
the songs of hallelujah sung
from far away, cause we won't come
too near, to see or ever hear

those word were spoken without tears
or fear of anything that lives
to die, or dies to live again.

On purple mountains where we blame

the sons of Old Saint Nicholas
for being, and doing just what comes
so natural that we all run

the way that we are told to do
and taught by experts who are from
that place where all men seem to lie

and die for things that they don't know

or care about, though it does only
grow inside once you divine
the way to tell these truths from lies.

Are, are exposed each time we care
to go away from all the rest.
Made free once we decide that She

the silent One, where all belong
in light built houses that don't stay
in motion pictures that are thus

creations of the Ones we bus

both forth and back behind the bar.
Set high enough to make us soar
in dreams that do not scare no more.

The Ones discovered it is far
more easy to be still, and kill
the false ideas learned with skills

belong to all us boys and girls
when we first landed on these shores
that look so real and full of joy

that only Santa with his toys
would draw us in with smiles employed

to fool the innocents, and joy
in sacrificing all was won
our last life time, when it was fair

to watch from mountains tops were won

without the blood of sheep or goats
but all of them seemed to abide
in valleys filled with peace and joy.

Once they decided it was for
this reason that we'd all become
the mad men that attacked the land
'til finally without demands.

We realize that all the band
who died to live again, began
the journey out of potholes made

inside the road that lead away
from false belief that one day may.

No, must achieve the freedom born
of living dead as just a way
to fulfill dreams, the only way

to find the answer won't delay
that truth, that we all fear to say

until we find that silent nights
come easiest, once we obey
that inner voice which only stays

and says the words no man can hear
until he tires of living lies
and bows his head, and takes that sword

he thought he lost those first few days.
That Sword of Truth that always stays
inside, and guides you on your way

to intuitions once delayed

to lead you into hell.
That brings you into life again
to live inside of me.

The One Pretending

I'm burning up inside this skin
and I don't know where I have been
or where I came from out of time

that is no more, and never was
a way to tell these stories too

the one who follows and will do
the bidding of the One, who tells
these stories better than can nail

the truth a way, and let it be.

The only time that is conceived
to be the right way, and the means
to gain all glory, and pretend

again, for just a little while.

For long enough for all to see
that it is easiest for me
to go my own way, and to dwell
in ways no other being can be.

Cause you, and I, and even she
can't walk that mile in others shoes.
No matter how we wish to use
and take the blame to share the shame.

There's only One, that stands the test
of being me, like all the rest
of people dwelling in this place

composed of mist, and yet does taste
and smell, and cry to bye-gone days

that were the worse that I might dream

about a future cast in stone
by memories of past events.

The One pretending to be better
then just living in the moment
anywhere or anytime

is just the way the mind says I'm
the One, who mines this shop, and shows
the way he feels inside these bails

of straw and blood, with bone to hone

you into what you do believe
each time you're told to look, and be
what others say, and write for you.

Cause you're the pillar of this place
you think exist in time and space
but they're just constructs that are base

enough to let you go, and pay
another day, and to pretend
that none of this is real my friend.

Told The Tale

Who told the tale that I forgot
that Santa Claus and all his dears
were the Ones who brought us here

to places out beyond the sun

to places we thought would be fun
to live in shadows, and to run
and hide, because we could not tell

the lies from true, and truth from lies.

Those lies have got us so confused
to be told what we need to use
to be shown what we need to get

to bind that, all that does beget

a feeling of loss, and regret
to find that thing, that don't bring joy.
That never last, but give us hell.

To give them up, to trade them off
is all we can to gain the cost
of what the truth of life is, now.

It can't be bought, or sold for crowns
upon a head the same as mine.

We all are made by One divine.
The one and only source of all.
The only source that cannot fall.

The force that's called from silence Is.

The only place, or space that gives
not time to things, not time to blink
is only found in stillness is.

The only way to know for sure

is go inside yourself, and know
what's true for you, what you can do
outside of dream nightmares that tear

the Silence of the Lamb apart.

That way, we have a brand new start
to build again this house of cards
without those stories make us sad

about reindeer that fly about

as high as angel's wings can dart
in space less skies that we've devised
to prove that God must live up there

in space and time, the place
where dreams come true.

State Of Singleness

I wonder what it's like at night
to know that you are truly free

to express all that you could be
in days gone by, when you and me
were born into this world of form.

This place we live and have become

the idols on this walk of life
pretending it is full of strife.

Yet we, we stop and look inside

to known the truer way to go
and find in time all things do rhyme
in syllables to make you free

to know that visions can't be true
unless you give them your belief.

Until you see what cannot be
the true way, that reality
is formed by thought, that's given time
attention, and design to chime

in ways that show what you perceive
is best appearing in this life
in which you play the victim, spiced
or diced apart to make a place

for lies, and doubts about the form
that must appear inside this dream

dependent on what you've been taught
and bought beneath that Apple Tree
where we first thought that we conceived

the idea, separation's death
to life as One, which does conform

to the atonement which is born
in time, to prove the pace is left
or right, or leads back to the mess

absorbed by other minds that fell
into this pit of "I can't tell"
just who I am, or where I'm from.

Though once I did remember coming
into form, in time and space
to see if I could make new rhymes

without the truer way to know
and guide me every way I go.

And that is why this fog and mist
appears to separate like fist
might pound upon a drum to summon
up ideas that cannot come.

The forms might be seen as the One.

Appearance from which none can come.

For there's no division at all
once you become, once you do know.
Once all of you do realize
you're simply playing in the snow

with zillions of these tiny glows.

Like stars appearing in the night
appear to be in separate flight
yet all this light in truth, you know.
It all is seen as One, you know

that snowballs are a way to show
the flakes do come together, grow
into a ball that's all in One
and that's the reason for this show.

Mind Divided To Achieve

Just now I sit, and I do see
that life is finally achieved
in ways I never dreamed before

the middle eye was opened for

to show me ways no one can say
or know for sure if it is they
who cause this world to be perceived

through minds divided to achieve
a place where dreams always come true

but suppose you don't know it's you
who does the work, or takes his rest
in knowledge that it all is blessed.

Illusion that does take you where

you fear the most, or do not care
to fight your feelings one by one
because the books they teach, express

the views remembered from the past.

They must always be first, and last
experienced in time and space.

That place the mind does recreate

to give you all that you caress
to take away your golden day
to reap exactly what you've taught

deserving of the others lost.

Or so you say, through judgments voice.

The one that follows all the books
that give out rules, and laws for life
that not even the mighty might

open, for ever and a day.

For life was created to live.

To express opposites you fear
or should I say polarities

which show you where your vision lays
or has been sent, by those been bent
by past experience, that did test

the way it was before the core

of love was broken by those whores.
Who followed other peoples ways.
Who forgot how to follow that

which comes from deep inside of him.

Whose chosen ways and means that form
up all the true beliefs they have
from birth, through youth, which is the truth

before corruption takes its toll

to keep you bound inside the maze.
Where we are taught we all have sin.
Where we are told we never can

do good enough to please a God
who has no pity, and does stand

for judgment, that's his righteous way

to save us all from truth, we scorn
when we do not believe ourselves
in silent stillness, we think hell.

About the Author

Bernard Ballard published his first series of books of poetry in 2012. Titled "Twelve Words On The Invisible Man", It is an exploration of human life experience. Written in metaphor and allegory, it explores the nature of reality from a metaphysical point of view, which transcends the normal way of seeing life (intellectual knowledge gained by the limited perception of the five senses), as opposed to going within to that silent still place of peace, where transcendent being originates and allows manifest existence.

His next series of books, titled "Mediocratic Metaphysics" (2013-2015), examines ideas and concepts about the human experience, relating how the laws of quantum physics can be observed through these experiences and considers how ancient text, and teachings derive from mystical traditions, and form the foundation of many religious doctrines.

"A Fairies Tell" (2015-2016) looks at life through the eyes of the Witness. The non physical aspect of being which cannot be known through intellectual thought. He attempts to give a history of man's journey, from a beginning in time to an awakening to present moment awareness, as the highest reality attainable.

Finally in 2016 he began the publication of The Awakening Psyche. A series which examines how mind is the maker of this life experience.

It is the reading , more than the writing that brings your word out into the cosmos according to your intention, and that gift will reverberate through all time.

Every time you think you are not good enough, it is like a slap in the face to God.

Holding grievances is the opposite of God's plan. Letting go of the need for the approval of others is letting go of grievances. Preconceived notions of how we feel the world should be. What others should be, or act toward me. Let go of expectations outside myself.

Also by Bernard Ballard

2012

Twelve Words On The Invisible Man (volume 1) (A Children's Book)

Twelve Words On The Invisible Man (volume 2) (See Through Me)

Twelve Words On The Invisible Man (volume 3) (For the Awakening Child)

Twelve Words On The Invisible Man (volume 4) (Reality, A Dream in Time)

2013

Mediocratic Metaphysics (Book 1) (The Story Of Life)

Mediocratic Metaphysics (Book 2) (The Mystery Of Oneness)

2014

Mediocratic Metaphysics (Book 3) (My Story Of Oneness)

2015

Mediocratic Metaphysics (Book 4) (His Story Of Life)

A Fairies Tell (Book 1) (How It Came About)

2016

A Fairies Tell (Book 2) (The Journey In Time)

A Fairies Tell (Book 3) (Transformation)

A Fairies Tell (Book 4) (Initiation)

Psychic Awakening

The Awakening Psyche

2017

The Awakening Psyche -Book 2

The Awakening Psyche-Book 3

The Awakening Psyche-Book 4

Notes

www.ingramcontent.com/pod-product-compliance
Lightning Source LLC
Chambersburg PA
CBHW032210040426
42449CB00005B/532